CONTENT

THIS BOOK provides a selective examination o[...]
and contractions affecting the railways of S[...]
Yorkshire, featuring the main lines and branch[...]
closed, and those which survived in 1985/6. The[...]
below feature the stations of the principal centres, and their
associated routes.

British Library Cataloguing in Publication Data
Vol. 2 : South and West Yorkshire
1. Railroads —— Great Britain —— History
I. Whiteley, J.S. II. Morrison, G.W.
385'.0941 HE3018
ISBN 0–947971–08–4

Designed by Nigel Harris.
Front cover design by Phil Cousins.

Typeset and printed.
Printed in the UK by Netherwood Dalton & Co. Ltd., Huddersfield,
Yorkshire.

RONT COVER: On June 21 1961, Thompson class A2/3 'acific' No. 60520 *Owen Tudor* has just started the imb out of Leeds Central, towards Copley Hill, heading morning local train to Doncaster. The terminus at eds Central opened in September 1848, and on ctober 1 1849 the Great Northern Railway began nning services into the station from Peterborough and oncaster. The GNR main line to London was completed 1852, with through trains making the journey from eds to London in less than five hours. The contraction the railway network was accelerated in 1963 when the eeching Report was published and Leeds Central ation was subsequently closed on April 29 1967, when 1 its passenger services were transferred to the rebuilt eds City Station. Sections of the viaduct and embank-ent between Copley Hill and the former Central rminus have disappeared following redevelopment, ut this particular section of the trackbed still exists and used as a car park for iron and steel manufacturers oncasters Monkbridge Limited, as can be seen in the set picture taken in December 1985. *GWM/JSW.*

ACK COVER: The scene immediately north of Batley ation has changed dramatically during the 22 years parating the two photographs. In the upper picture, lass B1 4–6–0 No. 61062 pilots LMS 'Crab' 2–6–0 No. 2750 with the Heaton–Manchester Red Bank empty arcels vans on May 23 1963. The train is on the former NWR main line from Manchester, and to the right-hand de, disappearing above the rear of the train, is the rmer GNR line to Adwalton junction and Bradford, om Dewsbury and Wakefield. Diverging to the left is e short LNWR branch to Birstall, which was closed to assenger traffic as early as 1917. A plain double-track ction remained on June 12 1985 as 'Peak' No. 45140 assed with the 2.20pm Newcastle–Liverpool. *Both:JSW.*

PREVIOUS PAGE: The changing scene at Wakefield. In the lower picture, Riddles 'WD' 2–8–0 No. 90109 passes Wakefield shed on March 24 1961, with a long train of empty BR 16-ton mineral wagons. Built in 1882 by the West Riding & Grimsby Railway, the line from Wakefield Kirkgate to Hare Park formed a link between the GNR and the LYR Calder Valley main line. Wakefield was a major shed for freight locomotives east of the Pennines and the ten-road shed, seen on the right of the picture, was built in 1893. Although it was altered in 1930, the shed remained active almost until the end of steam on BR, finally closing on June 3 1967. TOP: the same viewpoint on September 24 1985, as class 37s, Nos. 37 134 and 37083 pass the cleared shed site with a Preston Dock–Lindsey oil train. A large amount of freight traffic can still be seen on this route, especially merry-go-round power station coal traffic. *GWM/JSW.*

OPPOSITE PAGE: The disappearing railway at Methley, which was located on the branch linking the GNR at Lofthouse to the NER/LYR, near Castleford. The line was opened for goods in 1865 and to passengers in 1869, when services started between Leeds Central and Castle-ford. Methley had the comparatively rare distinction of having three stations: Methley North (on the Midland route between Leeds and Normanton); Methley Junction (on the LYR to Castleford) ; and Methley South, pictured here. The 'South' suffix was added in BR days. TOP: LNER 'B1' 4–6–0 No. 61388 passes Methley South with a coal train, heading towards Castleford and Gascoigne Wood, on the NER line. On the right is the connection to the LYR line at Castleford. Methley South closed to passengers in March 1960 and the decayed remains of the station are pictured on January 25 1986, part of the station now in use as a private house. *P. Cookson/JSW.*

INTRODUCTION

DR. BEECHING has much to answer for — a sentiment which I am sure is shared by many railway enthusiasts. Certainly, he was responsible for closing a considerable number of lines, which at that time were considered uneconomic, in both South and West Yorkshire, and of all the lines proposed for closure at that period, former GNR suburban lines faired worse than most. Generally this was because the GNR lines had duplicated the earlier and less heavily engineered routes. Whilst none can deny that there was probably more duplication of lines in South and West Yorkshire than there was in other parts of the country, and indeed, many towns were served by at least two rival main line pre-grouping companies, some lines which could have served a very useful purpose in the years to come were lost for ever. As our roads become more and more choked under the sheer volume of traffic, it is now becoming generally accepted that some of these lines, which were declared uneconomic by Dr. Beeching, could have had a role to play in today's transport system. In fact, it is somewhat ironic that very recently several new stations have been opened in suburban areas in an attempt to alleviate the traffic problems on our already congested roads. It is also possible that had certain lines survived for a few more years beyond the Beeching era, they would now have become major tourist attractions. One line which immediately comes to mind in this respect is the extension from Ilkley to Skipton via Bolton Abbey. How pleasant it would be today to see a preserved steam locomotive pottering through this section of the picturesque Yorkshire Dales.

My first recollection of railways in what was then the West Riding of Yorkshire, was the line from Bradford Exchange to Halifax and on into Lancashire. I attended Junior School at Lightcliffe until the age of 11 years, and the School was prominently situated overlooking the station and the adjacent goods yard. Passenger workings at that time were generally in the hands of Stanier Class 5 4–6–0s and 2–6–4 tanks and the goods yard was often shunted by Aspinall 0–6–0s. It is hard to believe that in the 1950s between Bradford and Halifax alone there were stations at Low Moor, Lightcliffe and Hipperholme. The station at Lightcliffe closed in 1965 and the goods yard has now been buried beneath modern housing.

After leaving school I worked for a time in Dewsbury, the office being only a stone's throw away from Dewsbury Central station, which was on the GNR line from Bradford to Wakefield. At one time this was part of the dense network of Great Northern suburban routes in the textile district, and at lunchtime I used to enjoy seeing 'N1' 0–6–2Ts or 'J50' 0–6–0Ts tackling the climb to either Batley or Earlsheaton. Dewsbury Centr station was allowed to decay for several years aft closure but it has now disappeared during th construction of a new ring road and it is difficult even find the trackbed in places between Dewsbu and Wakefield.

One of my fondest memories of steam in the We Riding was the cramped terminus at Leeds Centr which often reverberated to the Kylchap exhaus of Gresley, Thompson and Peppercorn 'Pacific From Leeds Central there was a steep climb, pa Holbeck High Level and Copley Hill motive pow depot, which extracted every ounce of power fro the locomotive, be it on a local working or a hea express bound for Kings Cross. I well rememb looking forward to my half-day release from th office to Technical College, whilst I was studyi for professional examinations, as unknown to m employers this allowed me an occasional oppo tunity to have a morning on the lineside at Leed which I found far more rewarding than studying! was hard to imagine in those days that Leed Central would soon be but a memory, and today a trace of the station and most of the line to Cople Hill has disappeared as a result of the relentle march of redevelopment.

The former LNWR main line between Leeds an Huddersfield passes through Dewsbury, and th provided me with an opportunity to see Edge H 4–6–0s in the shape of 'Royal Scots', 'Patriots' an 'Jubilees'. This route still sees a considerab amount of Inter-City traffic, which is now haule almost exclusively by Class 45/1s and Class 47 Not far from Dewsbury is the Calder Valley ma line which, although it did not produce the glar orous motive power of the nearby LNWR route, d produce a constant procession of coal trains fro Healey Mills to Lancashire, invariably hauled l either '8F' 2–8–0s or 'Austerity' 2–8–0s. For sever years during the 1970s and early 1980s, a consi erable amount of freight traffic was routed Lancashire via Standedge, but following th reopening of the Calder Valley route after th disastrous fire in Summit Tunnel, this route on again sees a considerable amount of freight traffi mainly in the shape of oil trains and merry-g round coal trains. Most of the oil traffic is generate at Stanlow and the MGRs help to feed Fiddle Ferry power station. Class 47s and Class 56s ha now taken the place of the 2–8–0s, but at least th railway survives and is still hard at work.

Having eventually concluded my profession studies — which had been constantly interrupt because of my love of railways — I spent a sho spell working at the District Valuers Office Bradford. This office was also very convenient situated, only a short distance from the line in

THESE pictures illustrate clearly how not only the railway has changed over the years, but also the general environment. In the upper picture, 'Deltic' No. 55012 *Crepello* passes Lofthouse Colliery heading the 5.30pm Leeds–Kings Cross. The colliery closed soon after this picture was taken and, following demolition, the site was still being landscaped on December 11 1985 as an HST forming the 12.45 Leeds–Kings Cross passed by. Both trains are pictured approaching the site of Loftouse & Outwood Station, which was opened by the Methley Joint Railway in 1858 and closed by British Rail on June 13 1960. A triangular junction was formed at Lofthouse with the Methley Joint Line, but this line was closed to passengers on November 2 1964 when the intermediate station at Stanley also closed. The East & West Yorkshire Union Railway to Robin Hood and Stourton was connected to Lofthouse Colliery sidings and a very short-lived passenger service on this line was with-drawn as early as 1904. The line itself had been closed by 1966.
Both: JSW

orster Square station, which was consequently given considerably more attention than the properties which I was supposed to be acquiring for Local Authority redevelopment. The afternoon 'Carlisle ...ow' produced a variety of different motive power and during this period in the early 1960s there was ...ill a considerable amount of parcels traffic handled at Forster Square station. Sadly, all this has now disappeared, leaving only two platforms operational, for use on local DMU services.

Whilst I have derived a great deal of enjoyment ...om helping to prepare this book, it has nevertheless been a rather sad task in some ways. Certainly, modern stock and locomotives, including BR's impressive HST units, grace some of the local main lines and whilst the 'new generation' DMU trains maintain secondary services, it is also true that much of what I came to love about the railways of South and West Yorkshire (and indeed across the country generally) has been slowly destroyed. Regrettably, the process still continues, although in recent times there has been a welcome awakening of public opposition to what is happening, notably concerning the Settle–Carlisle line, and it is to be hoped that this opposition will have a constructive effect. Otherwise, who knows what else will have disappeared in another 20 years?

JOHN WHITELEY, Shipley, May 1986.

NORMANTON station was opened on July 1 1840 and was an important station on the Leeds–Derby route of the North Midland Railway. It was originally a joint station, the cost having been shared by the York and North Midland Railway, the North Midland Railway and the Manchester & Leeds Railway. It offered refreshment room facilities for long distance travellers and, having been re-built in 1871, had an island platform almost ¼ mile long. Just to the East of the station was the motive power depot which was originally opened in the early 1850's. It was primarily a freight shed and the hug concrete coaling plant can be seen in this picture take on July 2 1966 showing Class 5 4–6–0 No. 45080 passin on a mixed freight. The depot closed on October 2 196 and it is hard to believe that the lower picture wa actually taken at the same location. It shows No. 4514 approaching Normanton station on June 8 1977 headin the 1.58 Newcastle–Swansea. Normanton station sti exists, but it is but a shadow of its former glory. *Bot GWM*

MOST of my life has been spent in the area covered by this book, in particular the West Riding of Yorkshire, and helping compile it has therefore been very enjoyable. Nevertheless, it has forcibly brought home to me how many railway features, which I (and I'm sure many others) had once taken for granted, and which have now gone for ever. Like so many things in life, it is only when something has gone that you fully appreciate how much it was a part of your life. Notwithstanding that, I still derive much pleasure from photographing current British Rail operations and no doubt many of the photographs taken in the 1980s will be of historical importance sooner than we might expect.

My most vivid early memories of steam locomotives at work in Britain are at Glasgow Central during World War II, when I watched the dirty LMS 'Pacifics' arriving and leaving with their trains. One other occasion in particular stands out in my mind, and that was when in 1943 I was travelling from Leeds to Glasgow St Enoch, and the first rebuilt 'Royal Scot,' 4–6–0 No. 6103 *Royal Scots Fusilier* backed on to our train at Leeds City station. The locomotive caused me much confusion as no photograph could be found in my Ian Allan 'ABC' to identify it, and it was some time before I sorted out the mystery!

I lived for many years at Ovenden, about three miles out of Halifax, on the old Great Northern/ Lancashire & Yorkshire Joint Line, and I was therefore brought up on a railway 'diet' of GNR 'N1' 0–6–2Ts and 'C12' 4–4–2Ts, together with Fowler 0–8–0s, and LYR 0–6–0s. The memories I have of these locomotives thrashing their way up the 1 in 50 gradients will always remain with me and indeed, it was on the Holmfield-Pellon line that I first experienced the thrill of my first footplate ride, aboard Fowler 0–8–0 No. 49540, of Sowerby Bridge depot.

I did have a few years away from Yorkshire, when I lived for a time in North Wales and Worcester. In Wales I was lucky enough to see the last of the LNWR passenger locomotives at work, and I vividly recall the immaculate Worcester 'Castle' 4–6–0s, and the Hereford 'Hall' 4–6–0s, not to mention a few 'Saints' and 'Stars.'

My first job in Bradford offered little opportunity for railway activity, but this changed when I moved to Brighouse, near the Calder Valley main line. Fortunately, the lunch break coincided with the passing of the premier train of the day, the 10.30am Liverpool Exchange–Newcastle, and so I became well acquainted with the famous Bank Hall trio of 'Jubilees,' Nos. 45698 *Mars*, 45717 *Dauntless* and 45719 *Glorious*, together with the same shed's unrebuilt 'Patriot' 4–6–0, No. 45517.

In 1960 I joined what was then the National Cash Register Company, in Leeds, as a salesman, and this gave me considerable flexibility during the day, and I travelled extensively in the Yorkshire area. I took full advantage of this opportunity and managed to photograph most of the main line steam traction operating out of Leeds at this time, before the diesels arrived in late 1960 and 1961. The first examples of diesel traction we saw in the area were class 45 and class 40 types.

I was fortunate to make many friends on the railway at this time, and there was little of interest which occurred in daylight hours that I did not get to hear about, or as happened on several occasions, was arranged for my benefit. Probably the most unusual of all events was the time I received a phone call from 'Control' during tea one Saturday afternoon, informing me that a GWR 'Grange' had just passed Penistone and was en-route to Huddersfield. Knowing it was definitely not April 1, tea was immediately terminated and I was at Huddersfield station within 15 minutes to see the train arrive and witness the damage to the cylinder casings where the locomotive had struck the platform edges en-route!

After steam finished on BR metals my railway photography virtually ceased, apart from trips abroad and endless visits to the Keighley & Worth Valley Railway. I now deeply regret this period of inactivity, but in 1975 I purchased my Pentax '6×7' camera, which completely revived my interest, and I was soon back at the lineside recording the modern scene. Now, my photography is back to the same level of intensity as it was during the steam years of the 1960s.

Times today are very different for the railway photographer, compared with 25 years ago, when it was a very lonely hobby. Then, I could spend a whole day on lineside on the Settle–Carlisle line, or on Shap Fell and never see another soul all day. How different it is today! I do miss the past, in particular the railwaymen; the drivers and firemen at Holbeck depot who I got to know so well, and I was privileged to witness first-hand their skills in handling steam over the 'S&C.' Their everyday craft is sadly missed today. It isn't quite the same with High Speed Trains or class 47s, but one must look forward to the future, and not dwell too much in the past. The railways of South and West Yorkshire still have much to offer the railway enthusiast and photographer in the 1980s, and hopefully they will continue to do so for many years to come.

GAVIN MORRISON
Mirfield, May 1986

THE terminus at Bradford Forster Square was originally named Market Street and was built when the Leeds & Bradford Railway linked the two towns via Shipley. Passenger services commenced in May 1846 and in 1851 the Leeds & Bradford Railway became part of the Midland Railway. In the heyday of the Midland Railway, Forster Square handled services to destinations almost all over the country. Valley Road goods depot was situated to the Eastern side of the main passenger lines, between Forster Square and Manningham, and thrived as a general freight terminal. Gradually passenger services from Forster Square diminished and after nationalisation the terminus was used for handling a considerable amount of parcels traffic. By the 1980s the parcels traffic had totally disappeared and the once important terminus now simply handles local DMU services from one remaining island platform. One can but wonder how much more important Bradford would have become on the railway map had the Directors of the Midland and Great Northern Railways managed to agree on forming a link of a few hundred yards across the town centre, linking Forster Square with Exchange, thereby creating a through North-South route. In the upper picture, taken on October 25 1980, Class 25 diesel-electric No. 25 099 is leaving with the Saturdays only 1.28pm empty newspaper vans to Manchester Red Bank. The carriage sidings can be seen on the right of the picture and part of the Valley Road Goods terminal above the locomotive on the left. Little remains in use in the lower picture, showing the 1.50pm Bradford Forster Square – Ilkley DMU leaving on September 21 1985. *Both: JSW.*

THE first station out from Bradford Forster Square was Manningham, just over one mile from the terminus. The staggered platforms of the station are clearly visible in this picture of Gresley 'K4' 2–6–0 No. 3442 *The Great Marquess*, in charge of the RCTS 'Dalesman' special from Bradford Forster Square to branch lines in Yorkshire and Lancashire, on May 4 1963. *JSW*

ADJACENT to the station at Manningham was the motive power depot which hosted a huge variety of different classes of locomotive over the years. The MPD provided locomotives for services from Forster Square but it never boasted the larger, more glamorous locomotives. In the picture above, taken on May 15 1957, the two platforms of Manningham station can be seen connected by the footbridge. On shed are tank locomotives of Fairburn, Stanier and Aspinall designs, one of which is already in store, its chimney 'sacked over.' Manningham station closed on March 22 1965 and in the picture (left) taken on February 8 1986, it is hard to believe that a busy motive power depot ever existed on the snow covered waste-land in the foreground. *GWM/JSW*

9

Above: At Shipley the line from Bradford Forster Square meets the former Midland Railway route from Leeds to Carlisle, via the magnificent Settle–Carlisle route. A triangular junction was formed, but surprisingly, not until only recently was a platform provided on the Leeds–Skipton side of the triangle, and then only on the 'down' line. Stanier Class 5 4–6–0 No. 44993 passes Shipley Bingley Junction signal box heading a northbound coal train in March 1967.
Right: The signalbox still survives on September 27 1984 as Class 31s Nos. 31 426 and 31 446 pass with the 7.38 am Hull–Carlisle. In this picture the new platform can be seen, and the line into Bradford Forster Square (right) has been singled.
Both: JSW

FOLLOWING the death of the Rt. Rev. Eric Treacy at Appleby, in 1978, British Rail ran two commemorative trains to Appleby on September 30 1978. One of them is seen here (top), headed by Class 9F No. 92220 *Evening Star* passing Crossflatts in the rain. Until the 1980s there was no station between Bingley and Keighley on the Midland route to Carlisle. On May 17 1982, however, British Rail opened a new station at Crossflatts, which is barely one mile from Bingley, in a successful attempt to attract rail commuter traffic to Leeds and Bradford from the already congested Aire Valley roads. In the lower picture, taken on December 14 1985, a local DMU bound for Keighley pauses briefly at the wooden platform of the new station, which cost £78,000. *Both: JSW*

Right: In May 1850 the Lancashire & Yorkshire Railway opened a terminus in Bradford which was later to become Bradford Exchange station. The Great Northern Railway used a terminal at Adolphus Street until 1867, when a connection was built to the Lancashire & Yorkshire station which was then enlarged. It had a cavernous double-arch roof and was at the foot of severe gradients from both the GNR line to Leeds and the L&YR line to Halifax and Manchester. In the upper picture Brush Type 4 diesel-electric No. D1999, almost brand new, is leaving the former GNR side of the terminus, heading empty coaching stock back to Leeds. Part of the overall roof can be seen in the background.

On January 14 1973 the original Exchange Station, which then comprised 10 platforms, was closed and replaced by this new four-platform terminus a few hundred yards higher up the gradient, on the opposite side of Bridge Street. This new terminus is adjacent to a large transport inter-change which is to the left of this picture, taken on March 26 1979 showing 'Deltic' No. 55 014 *The Duke of Wellington's Regiment* with the 5.30 pm to King's Cross. The distinct change in gradient can be noticed towards the front of the train. The site of Exchange station is now used for car parking, following demolition of the terminus buildings. *Both: GWM*

Above: Stanier Class 5 No. 44807 is passing beneath the impressive signal gantry on its cautious downgrade approach to Bradford Exchange. On the extreme right of the picture in the distance can be seen the line leading into the former L&YR Bridge Street goods depot, which has since been redeveloped as the site of the bus and coach station. There was originally a tunnel at this point, from Mill Lane Junction, which was 'opened out' circa 1873, when the deep retaining wall on the left was constructed. In the lower picture a Leeds–Bradford DMU is arriving at one of the two island platforms of the newly-sited Exchange Station on May 11 1979. The station was renamed Bradford Interchange in 1983. *Both: GWM*

SERVICES from Bradford to Halifax, by the Great Northern route via Queensbury, commenced in December 1879 and by 1884 a route to Keighley had been opened from the triangular junction at Queensbury. For about half a century Ivatt Class N1 0–6–2Ts (introduced in 1907) were the mainstay of passenger services on this route and No. 69451 is seen (above) at Great Horton in the 1950s heading a train to Bradford. Great Horton station opened on October 14 1878 and closed on May 21 1955, when local passenger services between Bradford Exchange, Queensbury, Halifax and Keighley were withdrawn. A bulk storage depot has now been built on this site by Grattan Warehouses, and the company's car park and canteen now stands on the site of the station, (right). *John Whiteley Collection/JSW*

Left: The summit of the steeply-graded former GNR line from Leeds to Bradford Exchange is at Laisterdyke station which was constructed in a cutting and comprised two separate island platforms. One of these island platforms can be seen in this picture of Fairburn 2–6–4T No. 42283, passing with the up 'Yorkshire Pullman' of June 9 1967. Laisterdyke station was opened on August 1 1854 and closed on July 2 1966. *GWM*

'Deltic' No. 55012 *Crepello* passes the site of Laisterdyke station, heading the 11.55 am Bradford Exchange–King's Cross. In this picture the simplified and realigned trackwork is evident and on the left is the line forming the former GNR connection to Bowling Junction on the former L&YR route from Bradford Exchange to Low Moor. The remains of the footpath to the station can be seen above the locomotive and first coach. *GWM*

THE GNR took over running powers of the branch from Shipley to Laisterdyke Junction in 1871. There was a connection with the Midland Railway at Shipley, but a separate passenger station was built — much to the inconvenience of passengers. The line was originally built as double track but it was singled following the withdrawal of passenger services as early as February 1931. The line finally closed to all traffic in October 1968. Top: 'Jubilee' No. 45694 *Bellerophon* is seen on July 15 1964, heading an evening feight from Shipley to Quarry Gap Junction, Laisterdyke. Above: In January 1986 even the remains of the track bed are difficult to find at this location, near Fagley, where new houses now encroach on the once-open fields. *GWM/JSW*

IN 1850 the West Riding Union Railway opened a line between Low Moor and Bradford Exchange, a route which was later to become part of the L&YR main line from Bradford Exchange to Halifax and Lancashire. A line from Mirfield to Low Moor had previously been built by the West Riding Union Railway to connect with the line from Bradford, and a triangular junction was formed, in the centre of which were carriage sidings. This can be seen in the picture (left) of Fowler 2–6–4T No. 42406, shortly after leaving Low Moor station, heading an evening Bradford–Penistone local on July 7 1959. Local services between Bradford and Huddersfield (via Mirfield and via Halifax) were withdrawn on June 14 1965 when Low Moor station was also closed. The picture below of the same location was taken on September 24 1985 showing a Leeds and Bradford–Manchester DMU passing the abandoned site of the former carriage sidings, the majority of sidings already having been lifted. *GWM/JSW.*

IN April 1867 the Keighley & Worth Valley Railway opened a branch linking Oxenhope with Keighley, where it joined the main line which had been opened 20 years earlier by the Leeds & Bradford Railway between Shipley, Keighley and Skipton, which was subsequently to become part of the Midland Railway's route to Carlisle. In the latter-days of BR steam traction, the branch service was worked by locomotives allocated to Manningham motive power depot, and on June 3 1960 (above) Ivatt 2–6–2T No. 41326 is arriving at Ingrow, one of three intermediate stations between Keighley and Oxenhope. At the end of 1961 the line was closed by British Railways, shortly after which the Keighley & Worth Valley Railway Preservation Society was formed. After considerable efforts by volunteers the line was re-opened for passengers on June 29 1968, since when it has become a thriving tourist attraction in West Yorkshire. It boasts a considerable variety of motive power, and in the lower picture, taken on March 2 1986, Ivatt class 2MT No. 41241 is passing with the 1.10pm from Keighley.

Above: running under clear signals on July 1 1962 is 'Deltic' No. D 9001 *St Paddy*, in two-tone green livery with white cab window surrounds and small yellow warning panel. This position, between Leeds Central station and Holbeck High Level was a very good photographic location, though its appearance as a car park in December 1985 (left) made it hard to believe that famous trains such as 'The West Riding Limited,' 'Yorkshire Pullman' and the 'Queen of Scots' passed this way as they pulled slowly out of Leeds Central en route to London. Leeds Central was opened by the GNR in September 1848, and lasted until April 1967 whilst Holbeck High Level (just behind the photographer) opened in July 1855, closing in July 1958. *Both: JSW*

19

TO MANY enthusiasts who remember everyday steam traction in Yorkshire, the shed-codes 20A and 55A immediately conjure visions of the roundhouses at Holbeck and its famous allocation of 'Jubilee' and 'Royal Scot' 4–6–0s. Part of this well-known shed and the main line alongside is shown (top) as MR '4F' 0–6–0 No. 43987 passes Holbeck with an up train of vans and empty mineral wagons on May 21 1963. The massive coaling tower was a familiar and evocative landmark. Holbeck's steam allocation ceased on October 1 1967, but the shed remained open firstly as a diesel maintenance depot and then as a stabling point. The current scene at this location is shown (above) on December 10 1985 with a two-car DMU passing, forming the 12.43pm Leeds-Sheffield. Class 47 diesel-electric No. 47425 has been named *Holbeck* in memory of this fine shed. *Both: JSW*

MAY 1 1967 witnessed the closure of Leeds Central station as part of the rationalisation of the city's railway facilities, which also included the remodelling of Leeds City station, shown here. Above: On September 1 1962, LNER 'B1' 4–6–0 No, 61176 raises steam in readiness to depart with an East Coast excursion — note the attractive water column alongside the locomotive. Modernisation has transformed this location almost beyond recognition, as illustrated (below) as Class 45 No. 45056, leaves with the empty stock of the 7.35am from Bristol. *Both: JSW.*

22

COPLEY HILL motive power depot at Leeds was originally constructed by the Great Northern Railway, and it provided locomotives for both main line and local passenger workings out of Leeds Central station. It was situated in the triangle formed by the Doncaster and Bradford Exchange routes out of Leeds Central. The last London-bound steam hauled express left Leeds Central station on June 15 1963, after which there was little need for Copley Hill MPD, and its remaining duties were transferred to Holbeck shed at closure. Opposite page: The 9.41am Leeds Central–King's Cross service is hustled past Copley Hill shed on March 19 1963 by 'A1' 4-6-2 No. 60145 *Saint Mungo*, the train comprised entirely of BR Mk.1 stock. This was the last year of steam operation from Leeds Central to London, though No. 60145 survived a further three years, to be withdrawn from service in June 1966. The 'Pacific' was stored at York (50A) prior to being cut up for scrap at Draper's yard in Hull in September of the same year. Top: The last 'up' 'Yorkshire Pullman' passes Copley Hill, on April 29 1967 hauled by Brush Type 4 No. D 1548 (later renumbered 47433). The engine shed has been erased from the landscape, but the carriage shed is still in use. Above: The same location on July 24 1980, as No 47401 (subsequently named *North Eastern*), passes with the 10.45am Leeds–Kings Cross, the replacement train for the 'Yorkshire Pullman.' The site of the locomotive and carriage sheds carry new industrial developments while the 'up' sidings now exist in memory only. *JSW/GWM/GWM.*

SOME of the most dramatic changes on the existing railway network around Leeds have occurred at Wortley Junction, where the lines from Leeds Central and Leeds City stations met, and where trains crossed over to and from the links to Skipton and Harrogate. There were signal boxes on both sides of the line, together with some splendid gantries, as illustrated (top) on May 25 1963, as grubby Stanier '8F' 2–8–0 No. 48084 passed with a lengthy train of coal empties, bound for Stourton yard. The later picture shows Wortley Junction on December 12 1985, with a two-car DMU passing as the 11.10am Knaresborough–Leeds service. Major changes at this location prevented the later picture being taken from precisely the same position, and the 1985 view was taken from a position nearer to the gantry spanning the '8F's' train. The ten tracks have been reduced to four, most of the buildings in the background have been replaced and a dual carriageway has replaced the gas works and its rail link across the narrow street. Note the gas lamps! *Both: JSW.*

Left: The site of Garforth Junction, Leeds in March 1986, the signalbox, signals and diverging tracks long gone, and the surrounding countryside now occupied by housing and industrial development. It was a very different scene on June 8 1960 as LMS Class 5 4–6–0s Nos. 45233 and 45156 *Ayrshire Yeomanry* pass Garforth Junction with the Heaton–Red Bank (Manchester) empty newspaper van train. The Castleford branch can be seen disappearing off to the right and this lost its passenger service on January 22 1951. The link to Ledston, on the Castleford line, remained opened until July 14 1969 for freight traffic, this being originally part of the Leeds Castleford & Pontefract Joint Railway, which was subsequently taken over by the GNR. It was not possible to stand in precisely the same position to take the modern picture of Garforth Junction because of dense undergrowth. *P. Cookson/ GWM.*

LEDSTON is situated on the 6¾-mile line from Garforth to Castleford. The line was opened to freight on April 8 1878 and to passenger traffic in the following August by the Leeds Castleford & Pontefract Joint Railway. Passenger services were withdrawn on January 22 1951, but little has changed at Ledston over the years. The upper picture shows Holbeck 'Jubilee' 4–6–0 45593 *Kolhapur* running through the station on April 22 1967 with a special, whilst the lower picture shows the scene in March 1986. The section between Ledston and Garforth was abandoned in the late 1960s, whilst the rest of the line to Castleford remains open for coal traffic from Allerton Bywater Colliery *GWM*.

THE area around Wakefield Road signal box at Stourton, Leeds, used to be a hive of railway activity with a busy yard, wagon repair depot and steam shed to interest the photographer. The still-busy late 1970s scene is shown (above) on September 27 1979 with class 47 No. 47453 passing with the 10.31am Nottingham–Glasgow Central, in the days when main line locomotive hauled passenger trains still used this route. The signal box and its attractive gantries have since been swept away and the route is used in the 1980s only by DMU services, freightliner trains, using the depot on the right, and a few through freights. Class 40 No. 40152 is seen (left) at Wakefield Road in charge of an oil train from Stanlow, bound for Hunslet, on May 14 1984. *Both: GWM.*.

STANIER 'Jubilee' 4–6–0 No. 45647 *Sturdee* passes Newlay & Horsforth station, (top) between Leeds and Calverley, on April 15 1967 with a lengthy northbound mixed freight. Steam traction was drawing to a close on BR metals at this time and *Sturdee* was withdrawn from its home shed of Leeds Holbeck later the same month. It was cut up for scrap by Cashmore's at Great Bridge, in September. The station had been closed in 1965 and by this time the station buildings had been demolished. The platforms had been cleared by the time No. 40 192 was photographed (above) passing with a Healey Mills – Carlisle freight on May 14 1979. *Both: GWM.*

THESE two views of Calverley & Rodley are from the bridge which carries the Leeds ring-road over the Midland main line, and the changes have been dramatic. Little trace of the once-extensive carriage sidings can be seen beyond Class 25 No. 25048 (above), which was standing in for class 40 No. D200, on the 10.40am Carlisle–Leeds of September 23 1983. The class 40 was away at the BR Norwich Open Weekend. This was a much busier location on April 14 1961 as Holbeck shed's rebuilt 'Royal Scot' 4–6–0 No. 46113 *Cameronian* passes (below) with the up 'Thames Clyde express' on the up fast line, which was taken out of use in 1968. The station, which had four platforms (including an island) is visible in the background: it opened in July 1846 and closed on March 20 1965, when local passenger services were withdrawn on the Leeds–Bradford Forster Square–Skipton route. The carriage sidings, used to store stock until required for summer excursions, the signalbox, goods shed, sidings and loops have all gone today, leaving a plain double track section. *Both: GWM.*

THE railway at Otley was opened by the North Eastern Railway on February 1 1865. As illustrated in the upper picture, the station buildings were on the north side, and there was an island platform, with subway. Passenger services continued until March 22 1965, and all traffic ceased on July 23 1965. Stanier '8F' 2–8–0 No. 48352 is seen amidst much sad dereliction, performing the last rites of demolition on June 23 1966. Below: All traces of the railway have since vanished and the much-needed Otley by-pass has been constructed on part of the railway formation, the remaining trackbed lying unused in February 1986. *Both: GWM.*

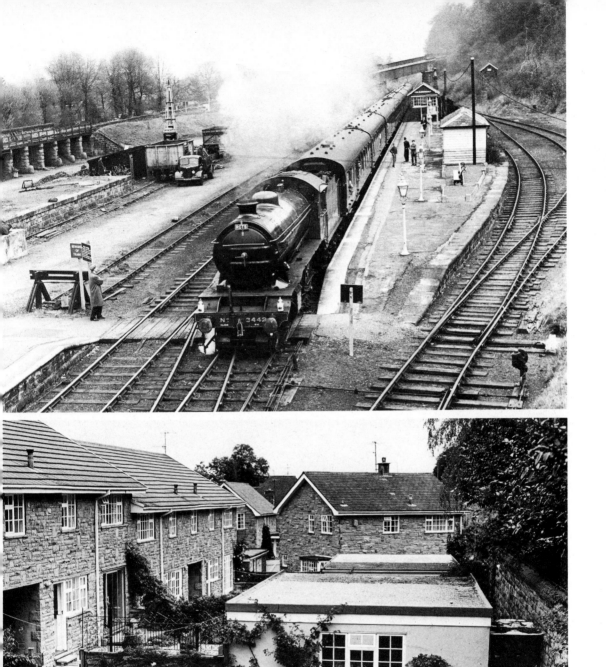

AT Poole in Wharfedale the change in the scene has been very dramatic indeed. The station was opened in February 1856 and lost its services, like Otley, on March 22 1965. The upper picture shows a most unusual visitor to the line, Gresley 'K4' 2–6–0 No.3442 *The Great Marquess*, which was hauling a RCTS special on May 4 1963. By July 1985 the site had been occupied by an exclusive residential estate. The bridge in the background in the upper picture carries the main Bradford–Harrogate road. *GWM/JSW*.

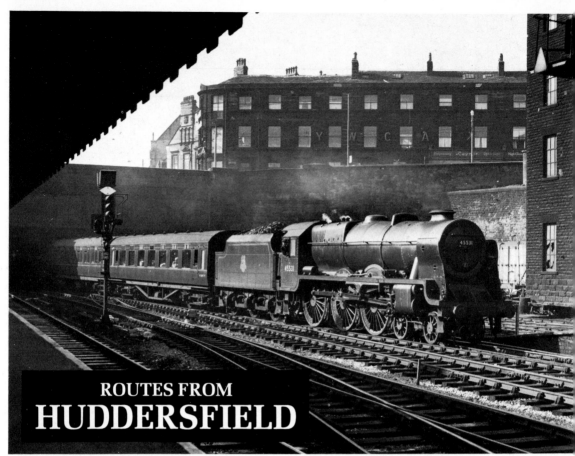

ROUTES FROM
HUDDERSFIELD

THE outside facade of Huddersfield station, opened on August 3 1847, overlooks the town's St. Georges Square and the station's superb 416ft long frontage has eight 68ft Corinthian columns and has smaller buildings on either side of the centre, with further columns. The station interior is less ornate and over the years it has not changed dramatically. Some minor alterations have taken place to the trackwork, and the bay platforms have been taken out of use, but the view looking towards the tunnel has altered mainly because the old YWCA building above has been replaced with a very modern structure. The upper picture, taken on September 27 1959 shows Edge Hill (Liverpool) allocated rebuilt 'Patriot' 4–6–0 No. 45531 *Sir Frederick Harrison* emerging from the tunnel with the 9.00am Liverpool–Newcastle express. Right: No. 45056 on a summer Saturdays-only Manchester–Newcastle train on September 18 1982. *Both: GWM.*

GOLCAR station was situated three miles from Huddersfield on the 1 in 105 climb to Marsden, en-route to Manchester. The line was quadrupled to Golcar by 1887, and Marsden by 1891, Golcar station being opened on August 1 1849. Passenger services were withdrawn from Golcar on October 5 1968, when the local services from Huddersfield to Manchester were virtually eliminated, except for Marsden, on the Yorkshire side of the Pennines, and Slaithwaite, which was reopened on December 12 1982. Top: Stanier '5MT' 4–6–0 No. 44772 leaves Golcar with an 'all stations' to Manchester on Saturday June 20 1959. Below: Passing the site of Golcar Station on May 13 1983 is class 56 No 56018 with a heavy merry-go-round coal train. *GWM/JSW.*

THESE pictures show the changes which have affected the railway scene on the Huddersfield side of Longwood, on the LNWR Manchester–Leeds main line. Top: A latter-day view on December 10 1981 as 'Deltic' No. 55009 *Alycidon* passes with the 8.50am York–Liverpool Above: The scene as it was on July 9 1966, as Stanier '5MT' No. 45005 passes with a Newcastle– Llandudno express. *JSW/GWM.*

SPRINGWOOD JUNCTION is located in a deep cutting about ½-mile from Huddersfield station, between the twin-bore Huddersfield and Gledholt tunnels, and is the point where the line to Penistone leaves the main line to Manchester. The 685-yard Huddersfield Tunnel caused many problems during construction and resulted in delay in the opening of the line. Situated in the smoky atmosphere between the tunnels was Springwood Junction signal box, which is shown in the upper picture of Stanier Class 5 4–6–0 No. 45204 piloting 'Jubilee' 4–6–0 No. 45563 *Australia* on a Hull–Liverpool express on May 23 1959. Just visible above the leading carriage is one of the two interesting signal gantries which were sited at the tunnel entrances. A new signal box opened at Huddersfield meant closure for Springwood Junction box and many others. The centre picture shows Class 40 No. 40086 passing the Junction, heading for Llandudno, with a summer Saturdays-only 9.00am departure from Scarborough, on July 4 1981. The lower picture, taken from the high bridge over the line, shows the rationalised trackwork at Springwood Junction with Class 40 No. 40012 emerging from Huddersfield Tunnel with a special working on October 20 1984 *GWM/GWM/JSW.*

BROCKHOLES, on the Huddersfield–Penistone line, was opened on July 1 1850 and at the time of going to press it was still open as an unstaffed halt, although under threat of closure. Above: A green-liveried class 101 DMU arrives at Brockholes, heading for Penistone in summer 1964. Below: The same viewpoint in February 1986, as a three-car DMU forming the 11.12am Huddersfield–Sheffield service, leaves Brockholes in wintry surroundings. The station building survives, but the water tank and column have gone, together with the lattice footbridge, siding, and gas lighting, which has been replaced with electric standards. *F.J. Bullock/JSW.*

THE short branch from Clayton West Junction to Clayton West was opened towards the end of 1879, its passenger service being retained until January 1983. It was a busy line which also served two collieries, one at Skelmonthorpe and the other at the end of the line at Clayton West. Whilst the collieries remained open the branch was safe, but their closure sealed its fate. Top: Class 37 No. 37040 is seen shunting Clayton West yard on August 5 1977, shortly before the colliery closed. By May 1986 (above) the railway had been utterly erased from the landscape. *Both: GWM.*

IT IS pleasant to be able to show a scene where the railway has actually re-opened a station in recent years, although not on its original site, at Deighton, on the Leeds side of Huddersfield on the LNWR main line from Manchester to Leeds. Right: Kirkburton Junction as it was on September 7 1968 with 'A3' 4–6–2 No. 4472 *Flying Scotsman* passing on a down special, complete with auxiliary water tender, with the line to Kirkburton on the left. Below: Deighton station was re-opened on April 26 1982 and on June 1 that year Class 40 No. 40077 arrives with a special working from Huddersfield to Bridlington — probably the first locomotive-hauled train to call at the new station. *Both: GWM.*

ONE OF the many branches once found around Huddersfield was the Kirkburton branch, which left the LNWR main line at Deighton. The branch was opened on October 7 1867, but the passenger service was an early withdrawal in 1930. The pick-up freight traffic continued for another 35 years but eventually the line was closed to all traffic on April 3 1965. Above: 'WD' 2–8–0 No. 90362, of Huddersfield Hillhouse depot, is about to shunt two loaded coal wagons into the yard, on March 30 1965. This must have been one of the last deliveries as the branch closed three days later, except for a truncated few hundred yards at Deighton, which lasted until 1971. It is hard to believe that a railway ever existed when looking at the modern scene (left) which shows part of today's residential cul-de-sac of modern detached properties.
F.J. Bullock/JSW.

BRADLEY JUNCTION and Bradley station, 2¾ miles on the Leeds side of Huddersfield was opened on August 3 1847 and closed on March 3 1950. The double track branch diverging to the right ran to Bradley Wood where it joined the Calder Valley main line, and where the local services from Halifax to Huddersfield used to travel, but these ceased in 1965. It was a very busy location until the early 1960's and on July 1 1966 (top) Stanier '5MT' No. 45295 passes on a passenger duty whilst 'WD' 2–8–0 90655 heads for Huddersfield with a freight. The station was located behind the signal box, but the site had been cleared by this time. The middle picture shows the current scene on March 7 1986 with a Class 45/1 diesel electric passing on the 10.05am Liverpool–Scarborough. The Bradley Wood branch survived as a single track link in 1986, but at the time of going to press it had no booked traffic. Below: The current view, looking from the bridge in the background of the two upper pictures, as 'Deltic' No. 55015 *Tulyar* passes with the special National Railway Museum train of coaches on May 21 1980 en route to the Rocket 150 celebrations at Rainhill. *F.J. Bullock/ JSW/JSW.*

THE EMBANKMENT opposite Mirfield locomotive depot has been a favourite location with railway enthusiasts for many years, as the LNWR and LYR main lines over the Pennines joined for the stretch between Heaton Lodge Junction and Ravensthorpe. Mirfield station, opened in April 1845 is situated to the top right of the two pictures between the mills, and is still open for passenger trains today. Shunting yards existed on both sides of Mirfield, although the west end was mainly occupied by the locomotive depot, which is just to the left of the pictures. The upper picture shows 'Jubilee' No. 45593 *Kolhapur* passing on a Leeds–Wavertree parcels train on September 19 1966. The MPD's water tower, coaling stage and sidings are clearly visible and whilst the depot closed in April 1967, the shed building is still in existence in 1986, in use by a local transport company. The current scene shown in the lower picture shows the first visit to the area of one of British Rail's new 'Sprinter' DMU trains, on January 11 1986. The second track from the right has been taken out of use and was due to be lifted as part of the reorganisation of Heaton Lodge Junction and Thornhill Junction. Note how the number of mill chimneys has diminished over the years. This section of track is famous as being the first to have the unique speed signalling system to be introduced in the country by the LMS in 1932. *Both: GWM.*

RAVENSTHORPE station is just a few yards to the east of Thornhill LNW Junction, situated on the LNWR main line to Leeds. It opened on September 1 1891, several years after Dewsbury Wellington Road and Mirfield, which are located on either side of the Junction. This extremely busy junction is an excellent vantage point to watch the trains pass and in the upper picture, taken on March 13 1963, 'WD' 2–8–0 No. 90326 is heading west, and at this location it was quite common to see two freights running side by side. The power station visible on the left is now out of use and during 1985 the junction was rationalised, as illustrated (above) with Class 56 No. 56074 *Kellingley Colliery* passing with a loaded MGR train for Fiddlers Ferry power station, in February 1986. Rationalisation of the junction has allowed the speed limit to be raised to 65mph. The station is still open although unstaffed, and is served by the Huddersfield–Leeds local service. *Both: JSW*

HECKMONDWIKE Junction was situated on the Lancashire — Yorkshire line from Low Moor to Mirfield and Thornhill, the lines to Mirfield and Thornhhill splitting at the junction. The Spen Valley line as it was known opened in 1848, although the branch to Thornhill was not opened until 1869. The Mirfield–Heckmondwike section closed to all traffic on June 14 1965. Above: On March 14 1963 Midland 0–6–0 No. 44408 restarts a freight for Low Moor, having arrived from Thornhill. In the background can be seen the LNWR 'new' line from Heaton Lodge Junction to Leeds. Below: The sad remains in December 1985, the track still in situ as it had been used until recently by oil traffic to a depot just to the north of Heckmondwike on the LNWR 'new' line. There are plans to have the line from Low Moor restored as an electric tramway as part of a tranport museum plan, but the reorganisation of local government has thrown this scheme into doubt *Both JSW.*

BRIGHOUSE was one of the four-track sections of the Calder Valley main line, the original two-track sec ion being doubled at this point by 1914. There were also extensive goods yards, as shown opposite, as Riddles 'WD' 2–8–0 No. 90016 passes on July 17 1960 with an empty train of 16-ton steel-bodied standard BR mineral wagons from Lancashire bound for the Yorkshire coalfield. The 'WD' 2–8–0s were a very common sight in this region on coal traffic, No. 90016 surviving until June 1967 , after which it was stored at Goole (50D) until October. It was scrapped by Albert Draper, at Hull, cutting-up being completed in January 1968.

Since the 'past' picture was taken, the goods yard has been closed and completely lifted, and the mainline has reverted to two-track operation. In the first half of the 1980s the only regularly booked passenger train over this route was the summer Saturdays-only Sheffield–Blackpool and return, and on May 28 1983 this train is pictured (top) at Brighouse with Class 47 No. 47213 in charge. Brighouse station — of which there are still a few remains — is just out of

sight around the curve in the top left-hand side of the picture. It opened on October 5 1840 and survived until January 3 1970. Above : A view looking east across this once extensive railway location, as Class 31 No. 31127 passes with the Saturdays-only Bridlington–Bradford Exchange of August 23 1980. The M62 motorway is in the background. *GWM/GWM/JSW.*

Top: Elland station, situated on the Lancashire & Yorkshire Railway Calder Valley main line between Brighouse and Sowerby Bridge, had an island platform. It was served in its latter years by Huddersfield–Halifax/Bradford locals, as well as trains from Normanton to Sowerby Bridge. Opened in 1841, it survived until September 1962. In the days when the Calder Valley line was heavily used by freight traffic it was the point at which the four-track section merged into two through Elland Tunnel, and the water tower was well-used by up freights pausing on the long climb from Wakefield to Summit Tunnel. On August 18 1958 Fowler 2–6–4T No. 42384 leaves with a Penistone–Bradford train (top), and as can be seen in the lower picture, little trace of the old station or track layout now exists. There is no regular passenger traffic on this section of the line, except a Summer Saturdays-only Sheffield–Blackpool train, although the route is often used at weekends by passenger trains when the Standedge route over the Pennines is closed for engineering work. The later picture shows Class 45/0 No. 45003 on September 12 1981, passing the site of the station with the 7.57am Weymouth–Bradford Summer Saturdays-only train, a working which has since ceased. *GWM/JSW*

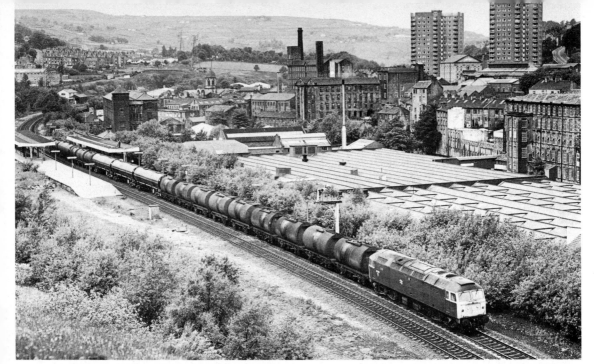

THE skyline at Sowerby Bridge has altered a great deal in the 25 years separating these two pictures. As is usual in West Yorkshire, the number of mills and their wide variety of chimneys have been drastically reduced. Sowerby Bridge station opened in 1878 and was the point where the 3¾-mile branch to Rishworth left the main line, and the tracks diverging to the left in the foreground in the upper picture led to the tunnel on the branch. Sowerby Bridge station had one island platform and a second platform, with bays. The site of the locomotive depot can be seen in the distance in the later picture, just to the right of the tunnel mouth at the west end of the yard. Above: No. 47380 passes Sowerby Bridge on June 19 1983 with a Stanlow–Leeds Hunslet oil train. The station is still in use but the once-extensive layout survives only as a plain double track section. Below: The view from a similar viewpoint on August 10 1958 as 'WD' 2–8–0 No. 90650 headed east on an unusual duty for the class — the Wakefield portion of a passenger working from Lancashire. *Both: GWM.*

EXCELLENT views of the railway can be obtained from the hills above Sowerby Bridge at both ends of the station. These pictures are taken from above the west tunnel and make a fascinating comparison over a period of more than 25 years, not only for the railway changes but also those affecting the industrial landscape of the town itself. Below the scene at Sowerby Bridge on March 15 1959 when the LYR locomotive depot was still open. It eventually closed in January 1964. The engine shed site is now used by a haulage company, and close inspection reveals that the water tower and coaling stage has been cleaned and converted for use as a garage service bay. The CWS mill beyond has vanished, as have the sidings on the right hand side, and the signal box is now out of use. The Calder valley line is frequently used on Sundays for diversions from the Standedge route. Opposite page: No 56109 passes with an MGR train from Healey Mills to Fiddlers Ferry power station, July 14 1986. *GWM/JSW.*

HALL ROYD JUNCTION, Todmorden, is situated at the East end of what used to be a triangle at Todmorden, where the Lancashire — Yorkshire Calder Valley main line was joined by the steeply graded Copy Pit line to Burnley and East Lancashire. Todmorden station is still in use in the 1980s but although local trains over the Copy pit line ceased in 1961, they were reinstated again in 1985, linking the West Riding of Yorkshire with East Lancashire. The Todmorden-Stansfield Hall section of the triangle was lifted after steam finished on British Railways in 1968, and some of the last steam duties on BR were banking turns from Todmorden over Copy Pit Summit. The upper picture shows 'WD' 2–8–0 No. 90181 on June 14 1961 heading for Burnley, taking the Copy Pit line at Hall Royd Junction. The banker will buffer up further round the curve. The lower picture shows the first 'new livery' HST unit at the junciton on September 25 1983 when it visited the Copy Pit line for promotional filming purposes. The site has not changed a great deal, although the signal box and water tower have gone, and this section of track is now controlled by Preston power box. Millwood Tunnel is in the background. *GWM/JSW.*

HALIFAX station was opened on August 7 1850, when it replaced the earlier Shaw Syke terminus. It was a LYR station, but its operation was shared with the GNR, and it was renamed several times over the years: Halifax Old in June 1890, Halifax Town on September 17 1951 and finally Halifax in June 1961. The station is shown (left) on October 1 1985, with a DMU standing beside the island platform which remains in use. Platform 3 has been without track since 1969. The disused platforms on the left formed the GNR part of the station and (below) on October 7 1967 LMS 'Jubilee' 4–6–0 No. 45562 *Alberta* is leaving with an excursion, whilst in the background English Electric Type 4 No. D 347 awaits departure. *JSW/ GWM.*

CHANGE at Holmfield. The line from Halifax to Holmfield was a joint venture between the Great Northern Railway and the Lancashire & Yorkshire Railway , opened for goods traffic on September 1 1874, followed by passenger services on December 5 1879. Holmfield was the junction for the Halifax High Level Line to Pellon and St. Pauls. There was a bay platform at the station for this branch, which was situated behind the trees shown in the upper picture. The line from Halifax to Queensbury via Holmfield, was steeply graded, mainly at 1 in 50, and abounded in deep cuttings, lengthy tunnels and viaducts. Top: Newton Heath Class 5 4–6–0 No. 45339 — very unusual motive power for this line — is in the yard at Holmfield, collecting the very last wagons from the yard on June 29 1960. Passenger traffic ceased on May 23 1955 but the freight continued for another five years from Halifax to Holmfield and St. Pauls, while freight to Queensbury and beyond ceased on May 25 1956. Passenger traffic on the High Level Line was short-lived, ceasing as early as January 1 1917. Above: The Smith Bulmer mill in the background is still active, but with fewer chimneys. Most of the site of Holmfield goods yard is now occupied by a small industrial estate and an electricity sub-station although the part of the yard where the picture was taken in 1960 is waste ground. All traces of the station have gone, except for the platform edging stones. *Both:GWM*

PELLON station and yard once occupied an extensive area, but to look at the location today (top) you would never know that the railway had ever been there. A few chimney stacks on the houses on the skyline help identify the precise site, but everything else has been swept away and redeveloped for industrial use. The view from the same spot was very different on Wednesday June 24 1959 (above) as Riddles 'Austerity' 2-8-0 No. 90122, allocated to Sowerby Bridge shed, waited to leave with a single wagon forming the 5.15pm freight for Holmfield. Opened to goods traffic on August 1 1890 and to passenger trains on September 5 1890, the line remained open for freight until June 27 1960, although passenger services were withdrawn as early as January 1 1917. The 'past' picture reveals that by 1959 at least the freight traffic was not heavy, but the island platform, out of use for 42 years, was still in evidence. The later picture was taken in January 1986. *Both: GWM.*

RAILS TO
WAKEFIELD

MOORTHORPE is situated on the former Swinton–Knottingley railway, which was opened in 1879. The station is still open and is served by a DMU service from Sheffield to York. The line was formerly used by North East–South West expresses until May 1984, when these services were diverted via Doncaster to Sheffield. There is a spur at the north end of the station onto the Great Northern Railway main line from Doncaster to Leeds, and main line trains from Leeds to Sheffield and beyond now use this route instead of the former main line. The upper picture shows a very dirty LNER Class K1 2–6–0 No. 62065 passing Moorthorpe with an up freight in 1960, and the current scene is shown (below) in March 1986, when the station buildings on the up side were being demolished, together with the signal box. *P. Cookson/GWM.*

Above: This delightful study, taken just south of Hemsworth, shows Class J39 0–6–0 No. 64979 (with a North Eastern Railway tender) heading a down coal train towards Wakefield on September 17 1958. The original line was widened to four tracks in 1912, when Hemsworth station was rebuilt as an island platform. Hemsworth station finally closed in November 1967, and as can be seen in the lower picture, taken in March 1986, the line has since reverted to two-track operation. In the present scene, South Kirkby Colliery has been developed in the background, although the colliery is not visible in the 1958 picture. The scene is soon to be altered again with the construction of gantries for the forthcoming electrification of the line to Wakefield and Leeds from Kings Cross.
P. Cookson/GWM.

PONTEFRACT BAGHILL was opened in July 1879 by the Swinton & Knottingley Joint Railway when a line from Ferrybridge on the NER to a point near Swinton (on the MR) was built. This formed part of a direct route between Sheffield and York, avoiding a congested section of line around Normanton which constantly caused delays to traffic travelling between the Midlands and the North East. The station is built on a curve as depicted (top) in 1960 showing Class V2 2–6–2 No. 60974 storming through with a Newcastle–Birmingham train. On the left can be seen the two bay platforms which were used as the terminus from the branch to Pontefract Monkhill. By this date one of the bay lines had already been removed but a variety of interest abounds in the shape of gas lamps, semaphore signals and a water column. Little of this ancillary interest remains in the modern picture (above) and the bay has been filled in since closure of the branch to Monkhill in 1964. Local services between York and Sheffield still call at Baghill station and the line sees a variety of freight traffic. In the later picture Class 47/0 No. 47115 is passing Baghill with a Southbound steel train on March 5 1986. Most of the station buildings still survive but the northbound platform has been reduced in length. *P. Cookson/JSW*

THE East & West Yorkshire Union Railway opened a branch in 1891 connecting with the GNR at Lofthouse and with the MR at Stourton, Leeds. For only nine months, in 1904, a passenger service ran between Robin Hood and Leeds, but the system was eventually to comprise a network of colliery connections around Robin Hood and Rothwell. The upper picture on this page was taken on February 20 1961 near Robin Hood, showing Class J52 0–6–0ST No. 68869 heading a coal train to Lofthouse. This line closed in 1966 and the remains of the trackbed are now almost buried beneath dense undergrowth as illustrated (below) in March 1986. The bridge carries traffic on the busy Leeds–Wakefield road and the Gardeners Arms does not appear to have changed a great deal in the last twenty five years. *P.Cookson/JSW.*

Below:The 2pm Wakefield–Goole train passes Pontefract Monkhill West Junction in 1955 as it approaches the station with Class 4F 0–6–0 No. 44458 in charge. The line diverging to the right was opened by the Wakefield Pontefract & Goole Railway in October 1849 and formed a connection with the North Midland Line at Methley Junction, via Castleford. It was just beyond the junction seen in this picture that the rebuilt Monkhill station was sited. The later picture (bottom) was taken on March 5 1986 from Monkhill station overbridge showing Class 56 No. 56005 heading an eastbound MGR coal train. Just out of the picture on the right is the Prince of Wales Colliery and the sidings are now used for the staging of MGR hoppers. *P. Cookson/JSW*

THE second station to be opened at Pontefract was Tanshelf, opened by the L&YR in September 1871. Tanshelf Station was closer to the town centre than Monkhill, and it was also very close to Pontefract Racecourse. 'Pontefract' was added to the station name in December 1936 and in addition to the two main platforms, a bay platform was also provided on the up side, primarily for special trains on race days. The bay and station buildings can be seen in this 1956 picture (top) showing a Sunday Doncaster–Leeds Central train which has been diverted because of engineering work and headed by LNER Class B1 4–6–0 No. 61326. Together with Featherstone, Pontefract Tanshelf was closed in January 1967 when services between Wakefield Kirkgate and Goole were withdrawn. In the lower picture Class 56 No. 56030 is passing the site of the station on March 5 1986 with an MGR coal train bound for Drax Power Station. The remains of the bay platform trackbed are just discernible and in the background can be seen the modern road bridge. *P. Cookson/JSW*

KNOTTINGLEY station was opened in April 1848 by the Wakefield, Pontefract & Goole Railway and early services from Kings Cross to the West Riding ran via Knottingley before the opening of the line between Doncaster and Wakefield. Knottingley grew in importance and the station was enlarged in 1854 at joint GNR and L&YR expense. It had five platforms and an overall roof, as illustrated (right) looking west in 1956. Below: Class 56 No. 56121 passes Knottingley heading a York–Drax MGR on January 28 1986. The imposing station which has been replaced by two short platforms sufficient to accommodate local DMU services. Knottingley still sees a considerable amount of freight activity, mainly MGR trains servicing the Aire Valley power stations. *P. Cookson/JSW.*

PONTEFRACT MONKHILL station opened on the same date as Knottingley, was the first of three stations serving the town, although Knottingley was subsequently to outgrow Pontefract in railway importance. The original station buildings on the up side were very grand in appearance and just after the turn of the century plans were prepared for rebuilding a larger station, but for a variety of different reasons work on the project never commenced. On March 5 1986 (left) Class 56 No 56029 approaches the station with an empty MGR train. It was a much busier scene in the mid-1950s as illustrated (below) as 'WD' 2–8–0 No. 90531 approaches the station with a train of westbound empty mineral wagons. Class '8F' 2–8–0 No. 48703 can be seen in the background in the down sidings.
P. Cookson/JSW.

WAKEFIELD KIRKGATE station was built by the Manchester & Leeds Railway in 1841 and rebuilt with an overall roof in 1857 by the Lancashire & Yorkshire Railway. Eastbound services from Wakefield Kirkgate serve Normanton, after which the routes to Leeds and Castleford diverge. To the west of Kirkgate is the main Calder Valley route to Lancashire past Healey Mills Marshalling Yard, opened in July 1963 after the existing yard had been enlarged to cope with the expansion of East/West traffic, particularly coal. Just to the east of Kirkgate station is a spur from Ings Road Junction to Wakefield Westgate station on the GNR line from Leeds to Doncaster. This link was invaluable as a means of diverting trains from Westgate via Kirkgate and thence back to the GNR route at Hare Park Junction. Above: On May 13 1962 the unusual combination of 'Schools' 4–4–0 No. 30925 *Cheltenham* and '2P' 4–4–0 No. 40646 pass through Kirkgate enroute from Nottingham to Darlington with an RCTS enthusiasts special. In the lower picture, the 09.14am Sheffield–Leeds DMU pauses at Wakefield Kirkgate on October 4 1983. During March and April 1972 the overall roof was removed and the buildings on the up platform were demolished. The up through line has also been removed, but fortunately the main station build-ing has been preserved, though it plays a secondary role to Wakefield Westgate. *Both JSW.*

Relatively few GNR lines survive in South and West Yorkshire and one of many railways to be closed following the Beeching proposals of 1963 was the passenger route linking Wakefield Westgate, Batley and Bradford Exchange. The original line linking Wakefield and Batley was completed by the Bradford Wakefield & Leeds Railway in 1864, but in 1880 the GNR completed the loop from west of Ossett to Dewsbury and Batley, which then became the main route. It was a very steeply graded line and (top) Fowler Class 4F 0–6–0 No. 44457 struggles up the 1 in 55 curving climb out of Dewsbury on March 29 1962. It is hauling a mixed freight bound for Wakefield and is about to enter the 179-yard Earl-sheaton Tunnel. On this route, both Dewsbury Central and Ossett stations closed to passenger traffic on September 7 1964 and in certain places all trace of this line has now disappeared. The lower picture shows the decaying remains at Dewsbury on September 23 1985.
Both: JSW

A 30-YEAR span of suburban pass-
enger traffic at Castleford station,
which was opened in 1871 by the
North Eastern Railway. The suffix
'Central' was added in 1952 to dis-
tinguish the station from Castleford
Cutsyke on the LYR route from
Pontefract to Methley. Right: On
January 25 1986 a BR class 141 DMU
forming the 12.04pm Knottingley–
Leeds service arrives at Castleford,
where reversal is necessary. This is
the only surviving route of three to
Leeds, the lines via Methley and
Garforth now having disappeared.
The NER box and the upper quadrant
semaphores at Castleford appear
virtually unchanged — apart from
the loss of one shunting arm — since
the earlier picture (below) was taken
on October 18 1958. GNR 'N1'
0–6–2T No. 69450 is awaiting a clear
road with a Castleford–Leeds Central
train. P.Cookson/JSW.

THE WHITWOOD MERE freight branch at Castleford served a variety of industrial premises from a connection at Whitwood Junction, near Methley. This was the pottery district of Castleford, but one of the largest industrial premises served by this branch was the Laporte Acids plant, part of which can be seen in the background of the 'Past' photograph (above) taken on August 22 1960, showing Class J72 0–6–0T No. 68726 doing some shunting. Most of the trackbed of this branch has now disappeared, as illustrated in the modern picture (left), taken on January 25 1986. Laporte Acids is now part of The Lambson Group and careful examination of this scene reveals part of the rear wall of one of the houses in a long-demolished terrace of 13 houses known as Britannia Row.
P.Cookson/JSW

THE ORIGINAL twin single track bores of the Woodhead Tunnel were opened in 1845 allowing considerable amounts of Yorkshire coal to be moved by rail to industrial Lancashire. There were often 40 coal trains a day over this steeply-graded route and electrification was first considered as early as 1926. However, it was not until 1936 that electrification between Manchester, Sheffield and the Wath marshalling yard was authorised by the LNER. In this scheme it was also decided to construct a new double-track tunnel at Woodhead, and in the upper picture (taken in September 1977) a westbound freight is just about to plunge into the 3 miles 66 yards new tunnel, which was brought into use in June 1954. The remains of the trackbed to the original bores can just be seen on the right. Right, above: Class 76 electric locomotives Nos. 76010 and 76022 have just emerged from the tunnel at Dunford Bridge whilst returning 'light' to the marshalling yards at Wath. Dunford Bridge station closed in January 1970, when passenger services were withdrawn between Manchester and Sheffield Victoria, leaving the line open for freight traffic only. Right, below: In March 1986, the remains of the vandalised signalbox were a sorry sight. *All: JSW*

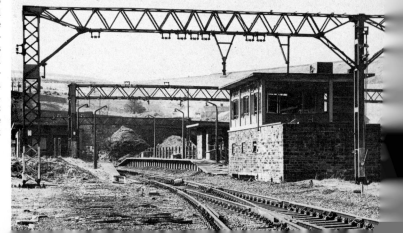

THE power supply on the Woodhead route was at 1500 volts DC with overhead conductor wires. In September 1977 (left, above) a Class 76 electric locomotive is passing Penistone station with an eastbound mixed freight. This particular locomotive was not fitted with jumper cables and was thus not capable of operation in multiple. Penistone was the meeting point of the Great Central Railway's Woodhead route and the route from Huddersfield via Brockholes, originally promoted by the Huddersfield and Sheffield Junction Railway, but opened in July 1850 by the LYR. Left, below: The platforms on the right are still used (at the time of compilation) by local DMU services between Huddersfield and Sheffield, but the decaying remains of the former GCR platforms can be seen on the left. The remains of the overhead electrification were being removed when this picture was taken in December 1985. The L&YR platforms can also be seen in the picture showing class 47/0 No. 47101 which has just arrived from Blackpool on June 23 1985.
JSW/JSW/GWM

Top: In March 1965 a pair of Class 76 electrics are passing Wentworth Junction with a rake of coal empties from Lancashire to Wath yard. It was from this point that westbound trains were faced with a rising gradient of 1 in 40 for almost 2½ miles to West Silkstone Junction — the notorious Worsborough Incline. Before the introduction of electric traction, four steam locomotives were often needed to work a loaded coal train up this bank, two at the front and two at the rear. It was for banking purposes that the famous LNER Beyer–Garratt 2–8–0 + 0–8–2 was built in 1925, and it was at this location that the bankers buffered up to the rear of the train. Assisting locomotives re-fuelled a few hundred yards down the single line which can be seen leaving the main line on the left, towards Levitt-Hag Colliery. This section of line, from just east of Penistone to Worsborough and Wath, was lifted by 1981 and the remains of the trackbed can be seen in the lower picture, taken in December 1985, together with some of the concrete bases which formerly supported the overhead supply gantries.
L.A.Nixon/JSW

STANDING at Lewden Crossing in late 1985, it was difficult to appreciate that the railway had ever been there. Following closure the track had been lifted and bulldozers were busy erasing the formation from the landscape. The modern picture (above) shows the crossing site in December 1985. Lewden crossing was situated on the Worsborough branch, between Aldham Junction and Wentworth Junction, near Worsborough Dale on the long climb to West Silkstone Junction near Penistone. Westbound freights were often 'banked' on this section, and on September 7 1977 (below) Class 76 No. 76051 is coasting downgrade, returning to the marshalling yards at Wath having banked a westbound coal train earlier in the day. The Manchester–Sheffield and Wath electrification was completed in three stages; firstly the 18–mile section from Wath to Dunford Bridge (completed in February 1952); secondly the section to Manchester (completed in June 1954) after which all Manchester–Penistone trains were electrically hauled, and thirdly the section from Penistone to Sheffield Victoria, which was turned over to electric traction in September 1954. In 1955 a short extension from Sheffield Victoria to Rotherwood Sidings was completed and in 1965 the electrification was extended to Tinsley marshalling yard. This scheme was Britain's first all-electric main line, but by the mid-1970s some of the non-standard equipment was becoming life-expired and passenger services had already been withdrawn from the route. It finally closed in July 1981. *Both: JSW*

UNTIL comparatively recently, Barnsley boasted two stations; Barnsley Exchange (opened in 1850) and Barnsley Court House, opened by the Midland Railway in 1870, with its branch from Cudworth. The upper picture was taken in May 1958 at Barnsley Exchange showing a variety of freight motive power in the shed yard which was adjacent to the station. At the south end of the station the level-crossing was controlled by Jumble Lane signalbox. The footbridge was removed when new crossing gates were installed. The lower picture, taken on March 6 1986, shows the 11.43am Leeds–Sheffield DMU leaving Barnsley Exchange, but all that remains of the old engine shed are the original brick-built offices, some of which can be seen in the left of the picture. In 1953 services between Barnsley and Sheffield on the Great Central route were withdrawn, and during 1958 and 1959 the shuttle service to Cudworth and also passenger services to Penistone and Doncaster were withdrawn. In April 1960 Barnsley Court House closed and services now use Exchange.*L.A. Nixon/JSW*

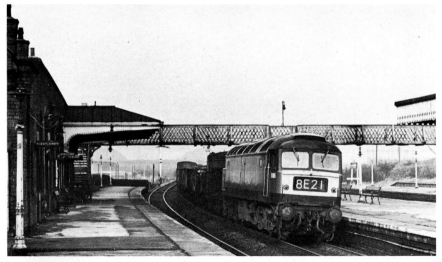

FOLLOWING the opening of the North Midland Railway route from Derby to Leeds through Cudworth, the Hull & Barnsley Railway reached Cudworth in 1885. A branch from Cudworth to Barnsley had been constructed by the MR in 1870, and Cudworth continued to grow in importance as the railways of South Yorkshire developed with the opening up of the coal fields and the establishment of heavy industry. Left, above: Brush Type 4 No. D1805 (later No. 47324) passing the not insignificant station at Cudworth with a southbound freight in the mid-1960s. Left, below: This March 1986 view from the same location shows a very different and desolate scene, only two through running lines now remaining. In 1958 the shuttle service between Barnsley and Cudworth was withdrawn and in January 1968 the Sheffield–Cudworth–Leeds local services were also withdrawn when Cudworth Station finally closed. The majority of through services have now been diverted away from this section of line, via Moorethorpe.
L.A. Nixon/GWM

Right: An overall view of Cudworth on Monday August 31 1982 as Class 47 No. 47510 passes with the 4.06pm Newcastle–Bristol service. At this time much of the extensive track layout and semaphore signalling were still intact, although all the platforms had been removed. *GWM*

20

WATH ON DEARNE was located on the former GCR route from the Doncaster area to Woodhead, and its railway grew steadily in importance with the expansion in the movement of coal traffic, and in 1907 the very large Wath marshalling yard was built. It was in the Wath yard that a good deal of South Yorkshire coal was collected before being despatched via the Woodhead route to Lancashire. Although this route was electrified after national-isation, the overhead electrification never advanced to the east of Wath marshalling yard over the remaining section of this route. Opposite page: On March 25 1977, Class 37 No. 37120 is pictured near Wath Junction, just to the East of Wath marshalling yard on the former GCR route, which has just passed beneath the Midland Railway route from the north to Rotherham and Sheffield. The locomotive is heading a rake of coal empties which have been electrically hauled over the Woodhead route as far as Wath yard. Manvers Colliery and coking plant dominates the skyline and the modern picture (above), taken nine years later on Sunday March 2 1986, shows the realigned track layout and the remains of the coking plant, which was taken out of service in 1980. The picture shows how not only the railway has changed in recent years, but also the surrounding landscape. *Both: GWM*

DEVELOPMENTS AT
DONCASTER

THE road bridge just to the south of Doncaster station has always been an excellent vantage point from which to observe activites around this important East Coast Main Line location. Top: On November 6 1960 an 'A1' 4–6–2 waits patiently on stand-by duty in the background as Gateshead shed's very dirty Gresley 'A4' No. 60016 *Silver King* sets out for King's Cross through the complicated trackwork. No. 60016, far from steamtight in this view, survived in service until March 1965 after which it was scrapped by the Motherwell Machinery and Scrap Company in May of the same year. In the early 1980s the layout at Doncaster was rationalised in order to raise the maximum speed on the through lines to 100mph for HSTs, and the much-simplified trackwork is shown (above) as class 47 No. 47115 heads south with a steel train on May 13 1986. The track on the extreme left is the Sheffield line; all tracks are bi-directional except for the two main lines in the centre. *Both: GWM*

THE railway and landscape on the 'London side' of the road bridge just south of Doncaster station have also seen many changes in the last 25 years. The railway today is spaciously laid out and on April 29 1986 (above) Class 47/3 No. 47361 *Wilton Endeavour* approaches Doncaster station with a down van train. The second half of the 1980s will witness the electrification of the East Coast Main Line through Doncaster. Below: It was a very different scene at this location on May 14 1963 as LNER 'K1' 2–6–0 No. 62066 steamed slowly north with a down mixed freight, flanked by the goods yard on one side and carriage sidings on the other. The scene is interesting not just because of the changes affecting the railway, but also those which have remodelled the skyline. *JSW/GWM*

ANYONE who cares about the future of railways in Britain would agree that they would rather see stations rationalised and retained rather than closed, but at the same time this pair of pictures clearly illustrates how much character has been stripped away from our railways as a result of 'modernisation.' Above: A westbound freight passes Thorne South (GCR) on April 17 1961, headed by Class 04/8 2–8–0 No. 63781. At this time the station had its own signalbox and ornate cast iron platform canopies. Below: Thorne South is still open in the 1980s, although it is now an unstaffed halt and the signalbox is long gone whilst the attractive canopies have been replaced by utilitarian 'bus shelter' style structures. The modern picture was taken on Thursday March 6 1986 as a two-car DMU arrived en-route from Cleethorpes to Doncaster. *P. Cookson/GWM*

WHILST the general appearance of Conisborough station has not changed radically over the years, it has nevertheless suffered from the contraction of track layout, signalling and buildings which have become common throughout the BR network. Conisborough's original station was opened by the South Yorkshire Railway in 1850, but it was subsequently moved to its present site, 0.2km west of its original position, in the 1890s. Top:

This was probably the only occasion that a Bulleid 'Merchant Navy' 'Pacific' visited Conisborough. On Sunday November 20 1966 rebuilt 'MN' No. 35026 *Lamport & Holt Line* passes with a Williams Deacons Bank Club excursion from Manchester to the north east. Above: The scene at Conisborough on Thursday December 12 1985, an unstaffed halt enjoying a very frequent service to Doncaster and Sheffield. *Both: GWM*

BLACK CARR JUNCTION, about 2½ miles south of Doncaster on the East Coast Main Line, where the Lincoln line heads east, used to be a splendid location for the railway photographer. Pictured here (above) is Class 47/4 No. 47553, in charge of the 11am King's Cross–Newcastle service on Sunday February 6 1977. Since this picture was taken the down slow line has been lifted, the signal box flattened and the signals cut down, leaving the location looking very bare. Right: On May 15 1986, HST unit No. 43053 races towards the camera at 120 mph, bound for Leeds, the electrification posts already in place on the down side to herald the next generation of ECML traction. *Both: GWM*

COMPLETION of the Woodhead Tunnel in December 1845 allowed through traffic to run between Manchester and Sheffield on the Sheffield Ashton-under-Lyne & Manchester Railway to Bridgehouses in Sheffield. With the increase in traffic a decision was soon taken to build a new station slightly further to the east and almost five years later, on September 15 1851, Sheffield Victoria Station was officially opened. It was opened by the Manchester, Sheffield and Lincolnshire Railway following amalgamation of the Sheffield Ashton-under-Lyne & Manchester Railway, the Sheffield & Lincolnshire Junction Railway and the Great Grimsby & Sheffield Junction Railway. Following completion of the 'London Extension' the Manchester Sheffield & Lincolnshire Railway became the Great Central Railway and traffic increased steadily as a result of the new link to Marylebone in London. In the early part of the 20th century, Sheffield Victoria station was enlarged and improved following development of the GCR cross-country services. The LNER sanctioned the Manchester–Sheffield–Wath electrification scheme in 1936 to cope with the ever increasing trans-Pennine traffic. The scheme was delayed by the war years and the electrification finally reached Sheffield in September 1954. Below: Stanier Class 5 4–6–0 No. 45208 is taking water at Sheffield Victoria whilst a Class B1 4–6–0 stands on the centre road, on June 19 1954. The station was closed on January 5 1970 when Manchester–Sheffield Victoria passenger services were withdrawn, and all remaining services were transferred to the Midland station. The decaying remains of the station are pictured (bottom) on December 7 1985, with only one track remaining to Wadsley Bridge sidings. *J. McCann/JSW*

THE
SHEFFIELD
AREA

AS THE coalfields and the iron and steel industry of South Yorkshire expanded, so the railways also continued to develop. The dominant railway companies in the Sheffield and Rotherham area of South Yorkshire at this time were the Midland and the Manchester Sheffield & Lincolnshire, which became the Great Central Railway in 1897. A degree of route duplication took place and in 1868 the MSL opened a line from Tinsley to Rotherham Central, which was extended to Mexborough in 1871. GCR services continued to thrive after the 1923 Grouping, but after Nationalisation in 1948 significant changes were made which were to have a fundamental effect on many of these services. The 1963 Beeching Report also advocated closure of a number of local services in South Yorkshire and in September 1966 services between Doncaster and Sheffield Victoria were diverted to Sheffield Midland via Aldwarke Junction, just north of Rotherham, and Rotherham Central closed. The remains of the northbound platform can be seen (left) in December 1985, but all the station buildings had by then been demolished. *JSW*

STANIER 'Jubilee' 4–6–0 No. 45593 *Kolhapur*, now preserved in main line running order at the Birmingham Railway Museum, Tyseley, passes the closed station at Rotherham Central in April 1967 with a rail tour comprised of BR MK 1 Stock. *L.A.Nixon*

WHEN the North Midland Railway constructed its line from Derby to Leeds, a route through Rotherham was chosen via Beighton which avoided Sheffield. Thirty years later, however, in 1870, the Midland Railway opened a line between Sheffield and Chesterfield which was to become part of the Midland Railway route from London to the north. A new centrally-located station in Sheffield was opened and this was originally named Pond Street, later becoming Sheffield Midland. In the early part of the 20th century, Sheffield had three separate routes to London; via the Great Central, the Great Northern and the Midland Railway metals. Although the Midland route was slightly the shorter at 158½ miles, it was the slower route of the three at this period, having a journey time of 3hrs. By 1968 this journey time had been reduced to 2 hrs 43 min and this was subsequently pruned even more with the introduction of the Inter-City 125 units. Top: The overall roof of the Midland station is prominent in this August 1952 view, with 'Compound' 4–4–0 No. 41191 standing at the platform with sister 'Compound' 4–4–0s Nos. 41119 and 41181 passing on the centre road. The overall roof was removed in the early 1950s and the modernised station can be seen (above) on December 7 1985, showing an HST standing on the 3.00 to St. Pancras and Class 45/1 No. 45123 on the 12.27 Leeds–Sheffield. *B.R.Goodlad/JSW*

Above: Ivatt 2MT 2–6–0 No. 46485 works steadily near Queens Road as it climbs out of Sheffield in September 1965 heading the 9.39am Sheffield–Chinley local service. Very little remains of Queens Road Goods Depot which was opened in June 1892 to cope with the city's expanding goods traffic. The expansion of both goods and passenger traffic was causing problems at the bottle-neck to the south of Pond Street station (later Sheffield Midland) and a decision was therefore taken to widen the entire line from the station to the junction at Dore & Totley. Included in this scheme was a burrowing junc-tion, which allowed down London traffic to cross beneath the Manchester lines, emerging on the approach to the station. This 1900-built dive-under can clearly be seen in the bottom right hand corner of the 'past' picture, but in 1971 work commenced on the introduction of multiple-aspect signalling which led to the removal of the quadruple track and the dive-under was taken out of use in June 1972. The later picture (below) was taken on March 14 1984, showing two HST power cars en-route to Derby. Work had almost been completed filling in the dive-under, on the left of the leading car. *L.A.Nixon/GWM*

CANKLOW motive power, depot was situated about 1½ miles south of Rotherham Masborough Station on the Sheffield avoiding line. It was not built until 1900 and was responsible for freight locomotives in the Rotherham area. It became one of the last Eastern Region steam depots after reorganisation, and official closure took place on October 11 1965. After closure it was host for some time to a variety of stored locomotives, and in the upper picture, taken in 1966, a number of LMS tank locomotives await their fate including (second engine from the left) the now-preserved MR 'IF' 0–6–0T No. 41708. The engines had been moved from Staveley, where most had worked in the vast Stanton and Staveley complex. The buildings remained in situ for several years, but the lower picture, taken in February 1986, shows a new housing development under constuction after demolition of the shed buildings had taken place for redevelopment. *L.A.Nixon/GWM*

TINSLEY marshalling yard was opened in October 1955 by Lord Beeching, and it covered an area of 145 acres with nearly 60 miles of track. In 1965 electrification of the Woodhead route was extended to the yard. Tinsley was designed to cater for 275 freight trains every 24 hours — that is one arrival or departure every 5½ minutes — but this degree of utilisation was never required on a regular basis. The shunting hump illustrated at work in the lower picture, over which the permanently-coupled Master and Slave Class 13s operated for many years, was computer controlled to give automatic control of wagon speeds with the aid of many Dowty booster/retarder units. Hump shunting ceased in October 1984 and as clearly shown in the modern picture (right) taken in February 1986 the installation has since been dismantled. The south-eastern end of the yard has now been abandoned, and the remainder sees only limited use, with many sidings used for storage of redundant stock. *Both: GWM*

84